LIGHTNING
BOLT
BOOKS™

Orange Everywhere

Kristin Sterling

Lerner Publications Company
Minneapolis

To my wonderful, lovable sisters. Thanks for sharing your crayons with me. —K. S.

Lerner Publications Company
A division of Lerner Publishing Group, Inc.
241 First Avenue North
Minneapolis, MN 55401 U.S.A.

Website address: www.lernerbooks.com

Library of Congress Cataloging-in-Publication Data

Sterling, Kristin.
    Orange everywhere / by Kristin Sterling.
    p.   cm. — (Lightning bolt books™— Colors everywhere)
    Includes index.
    ISBN 978-0-7613-5435-2 (lib. bdg. : alk. paper)
    1. Orange (Color)—Juvenile literature. I. Title.
QC495.5.S746 2011
535.6—dc22   2009038842

Manufactured in the United States of America
1 — CG — 7/15/10

Contents

Warm Up with Orange

Orange is bright. Orange is warm. Orange is an exciting color.

Look around you.

Orange is everywhere!

Owen and his dad lift a big orange pumpkin.

5

Orange can be found in the foods we eat. Families bake pumpkin pies for Thanksgiving.

Many kinds of fruit are orange.
You can eat oranges, tangerines,
and peaches.

Olivia loves to eat oranges.

Orange is found on large and small animals. Tigers are orange with black stripes.

This thirsty tiger slurps water from a pond.

Meow!

This little orange tabby cat loves to play with string.

Orange can be seen in nature.
You can collect orange leaves
in the fall.

Molly's bold orange hat matches the fall leaves.

The setting sun is a glowing orange color. What other colors do you see?

Orange is found in oceans as well. Clown fish dip and dart in warm waters.

Orange sea horses have curly bodies. Bright starfish have five arms!

This sea horse (left) and this starfish (right) both live in the ocean.

Shades of Orange

There are many shades of orange in the world. Let's look for a few!

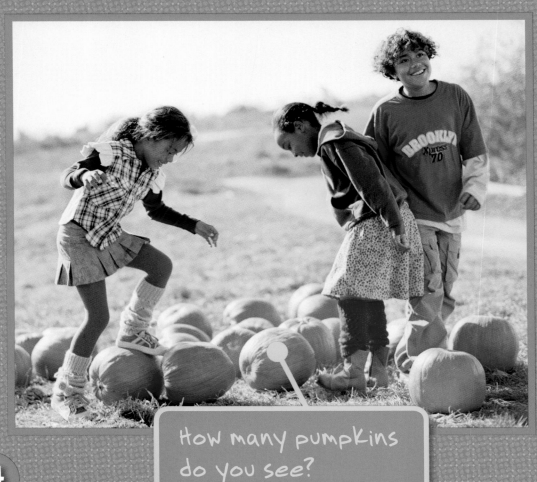

How many pumpkins do you see?

Peach is a soft orange color. This flower girl is carrying a peach-colored rose.

Safety orange is easy to notice. It is used on street signs and traffic cones.

Ollie drives a soapbox car between orange traffic cones.

Burnt orange is a brownish orange color. Danny camps out in a burnt orange tent.

Mixing Colors

Artists paint with many colors.

They mix red and yellow to make orange.

Orange mixed with white
creates a softer orange.
What would happen if
you added black?

Orange and blue are complementary colors.

They make each other stand out and look brighter.

People notice orange traffic signs because they pop out against a blue sky.

This bright orange sign stands out on the road.

Otto Loves Orange

Otto loves the color orange. He has orange hair and green eyes.

Pumpkin is Otto's orange cat. His favorite thing to do is sleep in the sun.

Pumpkin's fur has dark orange stripes.

Otto has orange walls in his bedroom. He takes naps on his comfy orange pillows.

Otto has fun at the beach. He rides an orange boogie board.

Crunch! Otto eats carrots for his after-school snack.

Do you like the color orange?

Make an Orange Smoothie

You can make this delicious, healthful treat with a little help from an adult.

What you need:

an adult to help you
a blender or food processor
½ cup milk
½ cup plain or vanilla yogurt
½ cup orange juice
1 peach, pitted and diced
5 ice cubes

What you do:

With the help of an adult, blend the milk, yogurt, and orange juice together. Add the peach and ice cubes to the mixture, and blend until smooth. Pour the smoothie into a glass and enjoy!

Fun Facts

- The largest pumpkin weighed 1,725 pounds (782 kilograms)!

- Carrots used to come in colors such as white, maroon, and yellow. In the late 1500s, people started growing orange carrots because they were more healthful. Modern carrots are usually orange.

- The orange blossom is the state flower of Florida. It is the sweet-smelling flower of an orange tree.

- Orange and black are traditional Halloween colors.

- The monarch butterfly has an orange and black pattern. The colors warn other animals that the butterfly is poisonous.

Glossary

comfy: comfortable, snug

complementary: completing or causing to stand out

create: to make or produce

exciting: something that makes you feel eager and interested

poisonous: filled with something that causes harm

shade: the darkness or lightness of a color

Further Reading

Enchanted Learning: Orange
http://www.enchantedlearning.com/colors/orange.shtml

Mixing Colors and Light
http://www.uvm.edu/~chmartin/sdeslaur/webquest

Ross, Kathy. *Kathy Ross Crafts Colors.* Minneapolis: Millbrook Press, 2003.

Snyder, Inez. *Oranges to Orange Juice.* New York: Children's Press, 2003.

Stewart, Melissa. *Why Are Animals Orange?* Berkeley Heights, NJ: Enslow Elementary, 2009.

Index

Photo Acknowledgments

The images in this book are used with the permission of: © iStockphoto.com/
cjmckendry, p. 1; Reflexstock/Rubberball, p. 2; © Jim Zuckerman/Alamy, p. 4;
© iStockphoto.com/digitalskillet, p. 5; © iStockphoto.com/Liza McCorkle, p. 6;
© iStockphoto.com/Donna Coleman, p. 7; © iStockphoto.com/Kit Sen Chin, p. 8;
© Roman Millert/Alamy, p. 9; © iStockphoto.com/Gennadiy Poznyakov, p. 10;
© iStockphoto.com/Imagedepotpro, p. 11; © iStockphoto.com/Don Bayley, p. 12;
© Carlos Villoch-MagicSea.com/Alamy, p. 13 (top left); © Buena Vista Images/Iconica/
Getty Images, p. 13 (bottom right); © Anne Ackermann/Taxi/Getty Images, p. 14;
© Maria Taglienti-Molinari/Brand X Pictures/Getty Images, p. 15; © iStockphoto.com/
Rob Fox, p. 16; © Stock Connection Distribution/Alamy, p. 17; © Todd Strand/
Independent Picture Service, pp. 18, 19; Reflexstock/PhotoAlto, p. 20; © iofoto/
Shutterstock Images, p. 21; © Joe McBride/Riser/Getty Images, pp. 22, 25; © Hartmut
Schmidt/imagebroker.net/Photolibrary, p. 23; © David Burton/InsideOutPix/Alamy,
p. 24; © OJO Images Ltd/Alamy, p. 26; Reflexstock/Image Source, p. 27; © iStockphoto.
com/MARIA TOUTOUDAKI, p. 28; © Brentmelissa/Dreamstime.com, p. 29; © iStockphoto.
com/Kim Gunkel, p. 30; © Thor Jorgen Udvang/Dreamstime.com, p. 31.

Front cover: © Chagin/Dreamstime.com (orange juice); © Navarone/Dreamstime.com
(clown fish); © Antikainen/Shutterstock Images (tractor); © Eric Isselee/Shutterstock
Images (Tiger cub); © Scott L. Williams/Shutterstock Images (basketball); © Valdis
Torms/Shutterstock Images (traffic cones).